D0243460

Network with confidence

How to make the most of your business contacts

Daphne Clifton

A & C Black • London

British Library Cataloguing in Publication Data
A CIP record for this book is available from the British Library.

ISBN: 978–0–7136–8146–8

Design by Fiona Pike, Pike Design, Winchester
Typeset by RefineCatch Limited, Bungay, Suffolk
Printed in Italy by Rotolito

This book is produced using paper that is made from wood grown in managed, sustainable forests. It is natural, renewable and recyclable. The logging and manufacturing processes conform to the environmental regulations of the country of origin.

Contents

How effective is your networking?

Answer the questions and work out your score, then read the guidance points for advice on improving your networking skills.

The idea of networking fills me with dread.
a) Constantly
b) Sometimes
c) Never

Networking seems pointless.
a) All the time
b) Some of the time
c) Never

I keep all my business cards and file them. . . .
a) . . . in a neat pile for when I need them
b) . . . when I have a spare moment
c) . . . immediately after an event

At a networking event, who do you take business cards from?
a) Everyone I meet.
b) Only those who offer cards.
c) People I want to keep in touch with.

At a networking event, who do you give your business card to?
a) Only those who ask for my card.
b) Everyone I meet.
c) People I think may be useful.

How easily do you remember people's names?
a) Very poorly
b) Quite well
c) Easily

How many networking groups do you belong to (online or face to face)?
a) Too many to count
b) 1–5
c) 6–10

When networking, how often do you listen more than talk?
a) Never
b) Sometimes
c) Always

How often do you review the value of the networks you belong to?
a) Never
b) When my boss tells me we have no budget
c) Annually

a = 1, b = 2, and c = 3.

Now add up your scores.

- **8–14**: Networking is pretty much a chore for you at the moment. There is a lot you can do to make it an experience that will really benefit both you and your business, so read on to find out how each chapter and its featured exercises will bring confidence and meaning to your networking.
- **15–19**: Your skills can do with some sharpening, so start to push yourself out of your comfort zone. The exercises in each chapter will stretch you further and take your networking to the next level.
- **20–24**: You're confident when you network, but there's always more to learn. Use the exercises in each chapter to affirm what you already do and then try some new techniques to make that stretch to greater success with your networking.

About the author

A passionate, energetic businesswoman, Daphne Clifton has a successful track record in the media world. This book comes from her desire to encourage others to live life to the full by providing an accessible grounding in what many people see as one of the most challenging areas of social and business interaction. For more information, visit Clifton Consulting online at: **www.cliftonconsulting.com**

Is there really an art to networking?

We are born to be networkers! From the moment we arrive in the world, we work out who are our most useful contacts—for food, warmth, love, affection, and so on—with no training at all.

If you feel as if you're *not* a natural networker, though, don't panic. There is a lot you can do to make the whole process less daunting and much more productive. We all work and communicate in different ways, but whatever our backgrounds and experiences, there is always an effective way for us to interact with others. We'll be concentrating in this book on networking for business, but many of the skills you'll learn will also cross over into social networking. Social networking tends to focus on meeting new friends or dating, while business networking is (as you'd imagine) geared towards finding new commercial contacts and customers.

Whatever the reason you're networking, communication is the key. This book will help you make the most of your contacts so that your business will benefit. We'll break down the sometimes woolly concept of networking into manageable 'chunks' that will enable you to build up your skills slowly but effectively, so much so that by the end, networking will feel like second nature to you! With that in mind, you'll find exercises along the way which will help you strengthen your networking muscles.

Step one: Realise you're part of a network *already*

So what is a network, then? The OED defines one as 'a group or system of interconnected people or things'. It sees networking as 'interacting with others to exchange information and develop useful contacts'. Sounds pretty doable, doesn't it? It is, and the first bit of good news is that you're already a part of many networks. These can range from your family, to friends, to sports teams, work colleagues, and so on, and are often called 'spheres of contact'. In fact, you've been networking practically all your life. When you were small, your networks developed through these spheres of contact. Immediate family is an easy one to understand. No matter how small our family, we see them most days; we interact with them regularly; we learn how to join in as well as how to love, fight, argue, and negotiate our way through the ups and downs of family life.

Exercise

This short exercise will help you to start thinking about your own spheres of contact. Taking no more than ten minutes, work from birth to present day:

✔ Think of your spheres of contact.
✔ Write them down, and don't worry about how many (or few!) of them there are at this stage. Make a list, draw a Venn diagram, a honeycomb or a spider's web—whatever works best for you.
✔ When you've exhausted the list, think about the following questions:

- With which ones am I the most comfortable?
- Am I comfortable all of the time?
- How do the spheres overlap?
- From which ones do I gain the most benefit?
- To which ones do I contribute the most?

Step two: Stop worrying about networking

Some people are natural networkers who love the prospect of making relevant introductions and enjoy the fun of a room full of new people. For others there is nothing worse or more terrifying. If you fall into this latter camp, take a look at the chart below. As you see:

- 40% of what you're worrying about will never happen and you won't make an idiot of yourself while networking;
- 12% of what you're worrying about can't be influenced by you anyway, so why worry?
- the good news is that there's a solid 8% that you *can* influence.

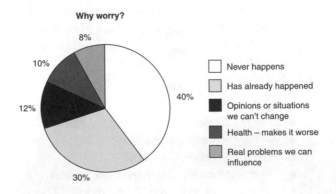

Why worry?

8%

10%

12%

40%

30%

- ☐ Never happens
- ☐ Has already happened
- ■ Opinions or situations we can't change
- ■ Health – makes it worse
- ▨ Real problems we can influence

Exercise

✔ What worries you the most about networking?
✔ Who can you discuss this with and ask for positive help?
✔ What can you do to overcome some or all of that worry?

TOP TIP

If you're concerned that your health may hamper your networking efforts—if you have poor hearing, eyesight, or mobility problems, say—don't give up: try to work round it. Be creative and don't be afraid to ask for help.

Take a few moments to think about what you hate and love most about networking.

- Write down your findings.
- Look at the list and consider which is your most effective networking activity. (In the 'return on investment' table in Chapter 4 you will be quantifying the benefits of networking.)
- Focus on the positive and think about what works well and how you can do more of that.
- What can you do to increase the amount of networking you enjoy that will also have positive effects on your business plan?

Step three: Define what 'successful' networking would be for you

'Successful' networking isn't the same thing for everyone. Some people may just want to learn how to approach a roomful of strangers at a party; others may have been told that an important part of their job is meeting new people and finding clients. If you run your own business, you'll want to let people know what you do, what you're good at, and why you're different.

If you've been dispatched to your local networking group to sell some widgets, hit your targets, and keep your job, networking can seem a particularly unattractive prospect. You need to decide what success 'looks like' for your networking and business and make sure that your boss gives you specific, measurable goals to aim for so that everyone is clear about what's needed. There's no need to follow the crowd; while you can always learn from others, only *you* know how to define success for you personally and in relation to your business plan.

If networking and its outcome are important to you, now is a good time to start being honest about your networking and the reasons you do it. You may find it helpful to do the exercise below and run through it with a colleague or your boss. Often, articulating what you're doing and how you're thinking brings clarity.

Turn to Chapter 2 for a more in-depth look at tying your networking activities closely to your business plan.

Step four: Take it one step at a time

You arrive at your first networking lunch to have a long list of attendees thrust into your hand, together with a name badge and a glass of wine that you have to balance while you make polite conversation. Now what do you do?

Make a plan! Have you ever watched wild animals hunting for food? They are organised, either as a team or individually. They wait patiently and run, fly, or pounce only when they are likely to reach and kill their prey. This is not to suggest that networkers share many traits with wild animals, but that preparation is key. Once you're in your comfort zone, you can start to meet your own success criteria.

There are several strands to the planning approach and it very much depends on the event you are attending. The principle is the same wherever you go: for example, you may be planning for a dreaded dinner party with people you have never met before. Work may mean vast amounts of seemingly pointless networking. However demanding you find this, I challenge you to enjoy it!

Step five: Keep it simple

If you remember that networking is about making connections and developing useful contacts, you can use such knowledge as a tool for your networking experiences.

Start off by learning to make simple connections if meeting strangers daunts you. Even though this book deals principally with networking in person, you can also meet other people online. If you're nervous or shy, why not start off there until you're ready to stretch yourself? Focus for the moment on what you can do, not what you can't. If you work on the basics of networking first, your confidence and effectiveness will build.

Exercise

Think back to the spheres of contact you listed in Step 1. Now have another look at how they overlap. Inevitably there will be another set of spheres touching yours that link with people in yours and their spheres. Let me illustrate what may sound complicated!

I used to help to teach football on a Saturday morning at my son's junior school. A common experience for many of us, and as I was a full-time, working single parent, it was about the only way for me to find out what really went on at school and meet other parents. Back to the football pitch – chatting with another parent at the end of the session, here's how the conversation developed.

Philip: *Oh, I won't be here next week. I'm off to Devon.*

Daphne: *That's a pity, we'll miss you. Whereabouts in Devon are you going?*

Philip: *Totnes. My mother lives there and I try to get*

> down as often as possible even though it's quite a trek.
>
> **Daphne:** Totnes! My sister lives there. I know what you mean about the journey; my parents live in Plymouth. I was brought up there.
>
> **Philip:** I'll be in Plymouth too, visiting an old friend of mine. I was brought up there too.
>
> **Daphne:** Which school did you go to?
>
> **Philip:** Plymouth College.
>
> **Daphne:** That's where my brother went. What year did you leave? (Seeing if I could make a date connection and link to my brother)

And so the conversation developed, I discovered that the friend he was visiting is a great friend of mine and we both knew that whole family very well but from different spheres of contact. My sphere of contact was the church I attended as a child; his was from the son of our vicar who went to school with him. Those spheres overlapped and came to life 30 years later.

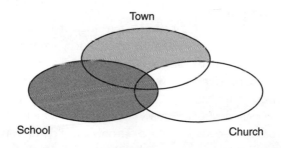

Town

School

Church

Have a look at the way I was able to make the connection:

✔ Open questions allow space for more than a 'yes'/'no' response (see Chapter 2 also).

✔ Once the location connection was made, I added in the people connection.

✔ The date could have been important; he might have known my brother at his school. He didn't, so I moved on to make different connections.

✔ I pushed gently at doors until one opened.

✔ Be encouraged! If you were looking for who had to do all the hard work—there was none needed!

At a networking lunch I asked for comments from fellow guests about what networking means to them:

■ 'It's about being part of the business community and helping one another.'
■ 'After last month's request to the group at the Chamber lunch, I've been given some office space, which means I can take on more staff for the charity.'
■ 'It's full of surprises! I was made redundant and within a week, the Chamber of Commerce had found me a financial adviser who really helped me out with my pension—it's worth 10% more now than I'd ever hoped for!'

Common mistakes

✗ You think everyone else is great at networking

Don't make any assumptions about others' effectiveness at networking. It's something that can strike fear into the heart of even seasoned business professionals. Remember, though, that we can all benefit from networking if we pace ourselves.

✗ You don't know *why* you're networking

Know what you want to achieve before you even think about preparing yourself to network. If you don't know why you're doing it, how can you measure how successful you've been? Read on for more information about tying your networking into your business plan.

STEPS TO SUCCESS

✔ Understand your spheres of contact in your personal world and then move them out, applying the same principle to your business

✔ Stop worrying about networking, and, if nothing else, remember you are in the same boat as many others when it comes to nerves and networking.

✔ Define what successful networking means for you and

your business. The clearer your focus, the more likely your chances of success.

✔ Build confidence slowly—take one step at a time and learn to enjoy the experience of networking as well as the benefits.

✔ Start by making simple connections.

Useful links

Learning-tech.co.uk (for mind mapping):
www.learning-tech.co.uk
Mind Tools:
www.mindtools.com

What's in it for me?

Before you start your networking campaign in earnest, it's helpful to think about what you're expecting from it. Having a clear focus and a set of specific personal or business goals will help you target the right people and groups in the first place, meaning that you can spend more time on making effective connections.

The 'What's In It For Me' factor (WIIFM) is usually high on any networker's agenda, for obvious reasons—you're engaging in it because you want to benefit from it in some way—but concentrating solely on what's in it for you can actually hamper your progress. On the face of it, networking can be viewed as a potential source of new business; a simple return on investment calculation (that is, have you earned more than you've spent?) can help you work out how much success (or otherwise) you've had. Of course you need to know why you are networking, but in order to benefit long-term from any network, you need to be contributing as well as receiving. With this in mind we'll now look at both these aspects of networking as well as some basic principles for networking conversations.

There are many pictures used to illustrate networking, and when thinking about the WIIFM factor, I find that of a rope the most helpful. Imagine a thick piece of rope in front of you: the individual strands have little strength on their own, but when they're woven together they can hold an oil tanker safely in port. Recognise the importance of each individual in a network, and you and your contacts will be able to make the most of one another.

Step one: Make sure your networking ties into your business plan

As our focus in this book is a commercial one, your networking must reflect what your business stands for, and where you want it to go.

Exercise

On one sheet of A4 paper, answer the following questions that relate directly to your business or the area of life relevant to your networking. The aim here is to help you see a picture of your business in one place and focus on the key elements.

1. What is your core business?
2. What percentage revenue growth are you looking for

year on year? (This could be a value rather than percentage.)

3. What other measurable success factors apply to your business? List them.
4. Who are your key clients?
5. Where do your sales leads come from? Write down the source and percentage revenue by source.
6. Who are your key target clients/markets for the next year?
7. How would your networking benefit from working more closely with your Marketing team?
8. List the current networks you belong to.
9. What do you enjoy most about your work?

Only *you* can answer these questions correctly, and you must be honest with yourself if you want to make the most of your networking and business contacts.

The final question above isn't a trick one. One of my challenges to you is to enjoy your networking. Part of that is about understanding who you are and being true to yourself in your networking, rather than imitating others. A counterfeit £10 note looks like the real thing in all respects but won't make it past the lie detector.

TOP TIP

Keep your A4 sheet of business objectives close to hand throughout the year. Refer to it monthly or quarterly to ensure you're on track and that your networking is targeting your overall business goals.

It's tempting to think that your networking has to work in its own right as part of your sales activity. In fact, networking needs to work *in conjunction with* your whole marketing strategy, which will include some or all of the following activities: your profile, branding, advertising, corporate positioning, promotions, and so on. If you work as part of a team, your networking is an opportunity to strengthen the connection between the various aspects of the marketing strategy. By implication, networking involves more than one person, so teamwork will be strengthened along the way. You'll come to see that there are internal as well as external teams operating. This can be particularly helpful if you work on your own—your networks begin to take on the appearance of an efficient team.

Step two: Ask yourself 'Why would *I* do business with me?'

Asking yourself this simple question is a great way of getting to the heart of your business, which means that you can put yourself in other people's shoes and work out what they can gain from working with you.

When you are networking online or face to face, you are representing your company as well as yourself and so need to be as professional as possible. Think about the points below so that you're not caught on the hop when you meet people at networking events.

1 The product or service you are promoting

- What is it?
- What is its unique selling point (USP)?
- What are you trying to achieve with it?
- How many do you want to sell/give away?

2 How you deliver information about your product

- Can you explain your product enthusiastically but (very importantly) concisely?
- Do you believe what you are saying? If you don't, why should others?

3 The person with whom you are networking

- Do you understand his or her product offering?
- Are you listening more than talking?
- Are you trying to make connections, no matter how small or apparently insignificant?

Step three: Be precise about who you want to do business with

If you've ever organised home improvements and decided to use a third party, you'll soon understand the importance of this section. Imagine you are going to spend £20,000 of your hard-earned cash on a fitted kitchen. How will you approach the project? Your plan will probably look something like this:

- Write list of requirements.
- Meet with three or four companies who appear to be able to fulfil your brief.
- Look at quotations and ask supplementary questions if needed.
- Take best and final offers.
- Make decision on who will do the work.

The last decision—deciding who you're going to give the work to—is probably the trickiest. It's unlikely that all offers will be the same, and you won't necessarily choose the cheapest option. However, if one company representative instils confidence in their product, takes time to listen to your requirements, and gets on well with you, then my guess is you'll choose that person ahead of the rest. They will be on-site for some while as the work progresses and you are confident they can deliver. You have made your decision amid tough, professional competition. People 'buy' people!

Networking for business is a commercial activity and is

based on making connections. Don't worry too much if it turns into social networking at points; as both centre on making connections with other people who are interesting to be with, it's understandable. If you are showing a genuine interest in someone's business, that will inevitably lead to non-work-related matters: where you live, family, and so on. In turn you'll develop a better understanding of how each other 'ticks', which will make for a well-rounded business relationship.

Moving on from straight work-based conversations to more personal matters doesn't jeopardise relationships; quite the opposite. For example, I'm interested in what people do outside of their working hours and how they balance work and life. In the same way that business relationships can point to out-of-work activities, you should never underestimate the benefits of social networking and how you can pick up useful work contacts for one another.

Common mistakes

✗ You're not focused

It's essential that you tie your networking into your business plan. While it's always good to get to know new people, you're doing it for the sake of your business, so you need to know what you want to achieve before you can work out a way to get there.

✗ You're selfish

As noted above, you want to network to improve your business, but you have to help others out along the way if they are to help you. Respect the contribution of others and be ready to help out where you can.

STEPS TO SUCCESS

✔ As the title of the book suggests, networking is an opportunity to make the most of your contacts. You can do that best when you are clear about your goals and organised with your networks. Each person will have a different style, so use the one that works for you.

✔ Keep your mind open to new networking opportunities.

✔ Let people know who you are and why you are there.

✔ Listen carefully and be genuine.

✔ Be sure that you are contributing to your networks as well as taking from them.

Useful link

Mindtools.com:
http://www.mindtools.com/CommSkll/ ActiveListening.htm

People 'buy' people

Many celebrities are used to advertise products and services these days. Supermodels and sports stars alike extol the virtues of hair products and anti-wrinkle creams; a former police commissioner endorses security products; and the late Thora Hird was regularly called on to promote products for those over the age of retirement. In the right context and to a targeted audience, advertisers know that people 'buy' people. Huge marketing research budgets go into finding out who trusts which celebrity and who will be the most effective name for promotional purposes. Next time you watch TV or read a newspaper, think about the faces you see and why they have been chosen.

One of the challenges is for you to enjoy networking and, if necessary, take the drudgery out of work. How many times have you been to a dreary networking event, with speeches that can't be heard and food that went cold about an hour before it reached the buffet table? If you've been in business for more than a week, you'll know that, if you wanted to, you could go to a networking breakfast, lunch, dinner, or golf day nearly every day of the week, including weekends—but what for? At around £20 per event (including membership fee) you are in danger of ending up with not much more than a lighter wallet and a heavier body, awash with full English breakfasts and vol-au-vents, but no relevant business contacts.

As we can see, many networking opportunities are available, and you need to work out which type or types work best for you. Some you may take to like a duck to water, while others you may find trickier, but that's completely normal. For example, if you work alone from home and are eager to meet people face to face, you may want to give Internet networking a miss. If you're going to make the most of your contacts, you will need to think carefully about your networking as part of a business plan. Spend some time studying what is available and what will suit you and your business.

Step one: Balance different types of networking

Whether you're networking online or in person, making the most of your contacts is a priority. There are many different types of networking groups; have a look at the following list. It's by no means exhaustive but it does show exactly why you need to strike the balance with your networking as well as remaining focused. The possibilities are endless.

Type of network	Face-to-face	Online
Industry body	X	X
Office intranet		**X**
Chamber of Commerce	**X**	X
Referral groups, i.e. BNI/BRE	**X**	
Local community groups	**X**	
Internet networking i.e. Ecademy	X	**X**
Professional associations	X	**X**
Membership of any club	X	X
Independent networking group	X	X
All our out-of-business-hours networks	X	X
E-networking community		**X**

X indicates that this is considered the primary method of meeting

Within the different face-to-face networks there will be a variety of formats. For example, some networks advertise themselves as 'referral opportunities', and the expectation is that members will actively seek and offer business opportunities for those within the group. Often, a group will have up to 20 members, with only one person from each business discipline allowed to join. At groups such as these, you'll need to commit to weekly attendance, and you may find that a strong, positive bond develops across the group. Other networking groups, such as Chambers of Commerce, meet monthly and there may be around 100 people there, with more than one person from each business discipline. I'm sure you can add to the list, and as you do, you'll quickly realise that the best way to stay focused is to strike a sensible balance between the type and volume of groups that form your business network.

Step two: Consider what type of networking events work best for *you*

If you're a nervous networker, be sure that you take simple steps in a comfortable direction when you're starting out. Build your confidence in one area before being tempted to strike out in all directions. Remember to bring a wider perspective than just selling your product or service to a networking group. For example, you may sit on industry committees that can help your group or you may bring useful contacts from your previous employment. Raising your company profile may be a high priority, and networking is just the way to do that.

✔ If you network online, keep your business objectives in mind and don't surf for hours on end just for the fun of it.

✔ If you work from home and enjoy face-to-face networking, make sure that you don't attend meetings just as an excuse to get out of the office (unless, of course, that's one of your business goals!).

✔ If your boss tells you to get out and network, be clear about why and how it benefits the business. Talk it through with him or her so that each of you understands the reason behind the networking. You may have separate agendas, and that's fine as long as they take you towards your individual and corporate business goals.

Step three: Listen

We all have two ears and one mouth. Using them in that proportion will help you whether you're a first-time networker or someone who wants to make the most of their contact base. Most nervousness comes from not knowing what to say; if you are listening, that won't be a problem! Active listening is an excellent technique to employ in all types of business environments, but it's particularly useful when you're networking. It involves letting the other person know you're listening carefully to what he or she is saying. You can do this in a variety of ways, such as: nodding; smiling; using approving phrases or words such as 'Aha', 'I see', or 'I agree'; asking relevant questions.

✔ Confirm your understanding of a conversation.

- ■ Summarise what has been said, and expected outcomes – then you both know you are in agreement and understand one another.
- ■ Start to think about how this person fits into your existing networks or if there is a new network for you or them to explore. Be careful not to go off into your own train of thought while they are talking to you.

✔ Ask 'open' questions which demand more than a 'yes' or 'no' response. For example, start with:

- ■ Who?

- What?
- How?
- When?
- Where?
- Why?

Step four: Understand!

So that you can contribute usefully to your network, you need to find out more about other people's goals too so that you can see how you can help them. If you don't understand what someone is saying or require clarification, have the confidence to ask. For example, use questions such as:

- Tell me more about . . .
- What did you mean by . . .
- I didn't hear what you said about . . .

It's also helpful to summarise your understanding of what the other person is saying ('So you feel that the council hasn't been pulling its weight?'). They can then put you straight if you've got the wrong end of the stick.

Step five: Engage your brain

Now that you understand your goals as well as those of the other person, you can start to engage your networks. (Remember the conversation in Chapter 1 that showed a 30-year-old network coming into play.) If you've listened carefully and understood what is being said or requested, you can think on your feet and make relevant suggestions.

■ How can you help this person to meet their goal?
■ How can this person help me to reach my goal?
■ Are there other networks that will help us both?
■ Agree a positive outcome or action for the future.

TOP TIP

When gathering information, learn to sort the wheat from the chaff. Keep what you will find useful for your business and discard the rest.

Step six: Be genuine

There's nothing worse than talking to someone who spends their time looking over your shoulder to see the next person they want to meet. Conversely, you are networking for a purpose, and if there is no mutual benefit or understanding from a conversation, it's time to move on. You can always come back later when you've had some space to think.

Be honest about how a contact may develop. There's no point in either party pretending that there is a basis for a sound business relationship when you've only just met. It could be considered clutching at straws but I think the following example is one way of taking the conversation forward honestly: 'I'm not sure what synergies we'll have, but the point about pricing sounds an interesting one to pursue. What do you think?' Relationships take time to build—be patient as well as genuine.

What can I contribute to my networks?

We each have skills to bring to any network as well as our own business needs to meet. With your long-term networking goals in mind, think about how you can contribute to each network you belong to. Of course, there may be some groups you attend specifically for supportive purposes, and that's fine. If you don't know how to contribute, think about the following ideas and add your own:

- Bringing new businesses to the group
- Working on the committee
- Writing articles for the group newsletter or magazine
- Offering a venue for a meeting
- Volunteering to speak on your specialist subject
- Providing signing or translations for the speeches
- Offering member deals and discounts on products or services

Exercise

Return to the A4 sheet of paper you completed at the beginning of chapter 2 and review what you've written against what you've now learned. Ask yourself: Which of my networking groups are relevant to my business goals? Who can I work with to improve and widen the benefits of my networking?

Common mistakes

✗ You try to run before you can walk

If you're new to networking, start off small and work up to more intense activity. If you prefer working online, do that first but plan to introduce face-to-face networking in X months' time (and stick to it!) so that you'll eventually benefit from both types.

✗ You don't listen

When you're listening to others, remember that you are supposed to be taking in what they're saying, not just waiting for them to stop speaking so that you can start. Show that you're paying attention by using the active listening techniques described above and by asking open questions that encourage a good dialogue.

STEPS TO SUCCESS

✔ Strike a sensible balance with your networking events, ensuring that they fit your business strategy.

✔ Discover what works for you and do more of it!

✔ Build confidence gradually and try creative new ways of networking as your confidence grows.

✔ Listen carefully to what others say about their business and networking.

✔ Remain focused at each event. Know your target audience and the product or service you are promoting in any particular month.

Useful links

Mindtools.com:
www.mindtools.com/CommSkll/ActiveListening.htm
The Myers & Briggs Foundation:
www.myersbriggs.org

Logical networking

Networking needn't be complicated, but you do need to be organised to get the best results. It's important to create and maintain momentum when networking. If you rely on others to contact you, you may wait for ever, so have systems in place to manage your time and contact details.

Step one: Prepare using the Pareto Principle

In 1906 the Italian economist Vilfredo Pareto observed that 80% of the land in Italy was owned by 20% of the population. Later, he noticed that this ratio seemed to apply to other parts of life too, such as gardening: 80% of his peas were produced by 20% of the pea pods. Over time, this concept has come to be known as the 'Pareto Principle' or the '80/20' rule.

Here are some 80/20 rule applications:

- Do 20% of your sales force produce 80% of your revenues?
- Do 20% of your products account for 80% of your sales?
- Do 80% of your visitors see only 20% of your Web site pages?

The Pareto Principle

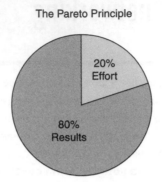

Good planning and preparation are vital for effective networking. Use the Pareto Principle to evaluate your client base and you will probably discover that 80% of your revenue is generated from 20% of your clients. Conversely, 20% of your clients may be taking up 80% of your time and preventing you from focusing on the priority areas that will enable you to reach your business goals by the agreed date.

Of course, networking isn't just about going out to events or joining online groups; you already have your own spheres of contact and existing business contacts. Are they working hard for you? Networking can't exist in a vacuum; you need to see it as a part, albeit an important one, of your whole business and marketing strategy. The earlier illustration of individual cords being stronger when intertwined as a rope is a good one here: each department and activity working towards a common goal will be far more effective than just one person networking like mad and becoming frustrated at a lack of results.

Step two: Analyse your business

To make sure that your business is getting the benefit from
your contacts, get organised and understand:

■ Who your contacts are
■ How they contribute to your daily activities and revenue.

Tempting though it is, don't let the WIIFM factor take over. It
is a two-way street and you need to contribute to your
contacts' business if they're going to contribute to yours.
How can you do that most effectively?

Exercise

Look at your business base and see how the 80/20 rule
applies. You can then focus your efforts in the areas that
will produce results. If this exercise sounds like the most
boring task on the planet, ask your accountant or
financial director to help you. It'll be right up their street
and they will undoubtedly throw new light on to your
business for you. Your internal networks—those who
work closely with you either in your team or within your
company—are as important as your external ones. To
establish how the 80/20 rule applies to your business,
questions you could ask are as follows:

■ Who are my top ten clients?
■ How much revenue do I generate across all clients?
■ How much revenue do my top ten clients generate?

- How much of my time do I spend on them?
- How many new clients have I generated in the past six months?

Step three: Review your existing contacts

Now is the time to review all your contacts. That may mean finding them in the first place, though! If you have an organised list already, that's great, but if not, make a concerted effort to sort yourself out now. Chapter 8 covers this in more detail, but, in brief, dig out all the business cards you've left mouldering in your bag, pockets, and desk drawers and make a comprehensive list that works for you. It needn't be expensive or over-elaborate, but you must have one: it will save you a huge amount of time and energy. You'll only be able to make the most of your contacts if you know who they are and how best to get in touch with them.

Exercise

Depending on how big your contacts list is, you may need up to half a day for this particular exercise. Work with another person if you can and use it as an opportunity to brainstorm—you will be surprised what helpful new ideas and suggestions an observant third party will come up with.

With your business plan (that A4 sheet from chapter 2) in the front of your mind and your contacts list printed out, find and mark the contacts who meet the following criteria:

■ Key clients—choose these from your measurables, such as how much of your turnover or profitability they represent
■ Target clients—short term
■ Target clients—medium term
■ Target clients—long term
■ Useful marketing contacts
■ Press contacts
■ Contacts you've lost touch with
■ Contacts you've never been in touch with other than first meeting
■ Contacts with whom you'd like to re-acquaint yourself.

Step four: Decide how you're going to approach each group of contacts

As time is precious, divide it up wisely between your contact groups. The key clients—those who are likely to bring in most money for your business, or provide you with the most valuable information—obviously come top of the list. Here are some suggestions about how to target them. You'll need to adapt them to suit your own business needs, of course, but it should get some ideas flowing.

Key clients

- Lunch/breakfast once a month
- Invite to quarterly corporate event
- Invite to relevant/new networking event twice a year
- Make sure they're on your mailing list (if they're not on there yet, you *must* ask their permission before adding their e-mail addresses)
- Annual review of business with board directors from both companies
- Ask to go on their mailing list for news updates.

Target clients (vary the following activities for the short, medium and long term)

- Corporate event quarterly
- Add to Top Tips mailing list, with personal contact first to explain and invite them to join the list.
- Provide competitive data monthly
- Sign up to their monthly newsletter—listen to *their* business needs and/or goals
- Find and meet decision-maker
- Pitch by the end of the year.

Marketing/press contacts

- Talk monthly on phone or face to face
- Provide editorial if requested
- Corporate event quarterly/annually
- Invite to networking event that is new to them—help them to expand their networks.

Lost touch or met once
- Contact ten per week to gauge their interest at being added to the Top Tips mailing list and establish relevance to one another's business for the future
- Move to target client list and book meeting
- Invite to relevant networking event
- Delete from contact list if appropriate.

Step five: Join relevant networks . . .

Having decided the approach you will take with each type of contact, you can now consider which networking events or activities will benefit your business plan. Remember that you have personal life goals too and bear those in mind when you're signing up for events; if you have family responsibilities, you may only be able to attend at certain times of the day. Be realistic about what you can achieve.

By joining relevant networks, you're creating positive momentum for your business as well as others'. If you have no idea where to start, look at the trade publications associated with your particular industry; there are bound to be opportunities for networking, even though they may be described as something else. For example, 'special interest groups' are often networks. Search online for websites associated with your industry and see what's on offer. Don't write off newsletter opportunities either; they often have details about industry events and networking groups, and the vast majority are free.

Exercise

Write lists or draw visuals that show your business networks in relation to your key and target clients, or, if that list is short, all your clients. Add in any networks that you belong to either face to face or online.

- Look for positive, active connections between types of clients or client groups as well as groups that have generated the most revenue for your business.
- See how many connections you have contributed to.
- Notice where your key clients appear.
- Look for emerging patterns that you can develop.
- Are there networks you belong to that are draining your resources and not contributing to your business plan?
- Which networks motivate you the most?
- What's missing?
- Who's missing?

Once you've collected together the information from this exercise you will have a much clearer picture of what sort of networks you need to support. If you're trying to break into new markets, have a look at their trade publications for information. There are bound to be groups and meetings that will take you towards your business goals.

Step six: . . . and leave unproductive ones

Taking the decision to leave networks that just aren't cutting the mustard is just as productive as looking for new and exciting ones. For example, how many networks do you belong to where you delete the monthly newsletter or put it in the recycling bin without reading it? Does this sound familiar? Then **unsubscribe!** Your time is valuable, so make the most of it. It was music to my ears the other day when a friend of mine said, 'I'm not sure if I'll join the group, there's a limit to how much I can do'. He is a brilliant networker who recognises the value of contributing to a group and doesn't want to join half-heartedly. He also knows the value of the groups he belongs to already.

The architect Mies van der Rohe brought to us the maxim 'less is more', and you would do well to apply that approach as you consider the groups to join or leave. You will be able to make the most of your contacts if you focus on groups that are relevant to your business. The logic will follow that you'll be able to contribute more to a smaller number of groups, and in contributing more you will receive more. Less is almost certainly going to mean more! Of course you need to be patient but you also need to be realistic and think about your networking budget and how far it will stretch.

Step seven: Measure the effectiveness of each network

If every sales director in the land had £1 for every time they were told, 'I can't tell you how effective this networking is, but I know it's worth it', there would be many more millionaires per square mile than there are now. Of course it's not always easy to evaluate or measure the effectiveness of a group, as there is a degree of subjectivity involved. The goal here is to add objectivity to the mix and relate the network to your business plan. By taking out the scattergun approach to networking, you also remove some of the subjectivity. I accept that we are all human beings, and for many of us, the human interaction creates a dynamism and momentum that is tangible but not necessarily easily quantified when it comes to evaluating a return on investment. Taking out the subjectivity for moment, think about the return on investment your networking produces. According to the US Government Accountability Office, return on investment (ROI) is 'calculated by considering the annual benefit divided by the investment amount'. You can work out for yourself the value of your networking by doing the exercise opposite.

Exercise

This exercise is a great way to become more objective about the real (financial) benefits of your networking campaign thus far. Draw up a table similar to the one overleaf, adding in items relevant to your business as you go.

Even if you decide to stick with the groups you belong to, at least you understand their value now. As with everything—review your membership annually.

Of people in business, 38% attend between 4 and 6 networking events per month, with a further 15% attending between 1 and 3 events. The costs accumulate rapidly, and building a chart like this will give you a starting point when assessing the value of the networks you belong to. It will also help you to plan budgets.

Step eight: Test the market

Formal networks that meet face to face usually involve some sort of annual subscription as well as a weekly or monthly fee to cover venue and refreshments. If you go to too many unproductive ones, not only will you be wasting time, but you may as well start burning piles of £10 notes for all the good it's going to do you. In addition, if you're a nervous networker, your confidence isn't going to grow if you spend a lot of time in groups that either you can't contribute to or from which you don't receive any benefit.

Networking group	Annual cost	Cost per meeting	Number of contacts	Revenue generated	% of sales	Subjective comments
Lunch group	£120	£14	234	£2,000	10%	• Editorial • Speaking events
Breakfast group	£400	£5	90	£1,500	7.5%	• Personal motivation • Editorial committee work
Breakfast group	£400	£5	65	£0	0	• Evaluate at year-end • Don't renew if no £
Online	Free	Free	75	£3,000*	15%	• Very time-consuming * This is one contract
Sports club	£2,000	£80	45	£10,000	50%	• Handicap down to 5 • Three new clients

The costs shown here are estimates.

Before you join a networking group:

- consider whether the group will deliver your target audience and help you to reach your business goals
- ask the organisers how often you can attend *before* making a commitment
- find out exactly how much it's going to cost you — networking is big business these days and you need to check that you'll be getting value for money, rather than lining someone else's pocket
- talk to existing members and listen to their view of the group and the value it brings to their business
- think about your time and how much you can *realistically* commit to such a group — don't sign up to three breakfast groups if a 5.30am start will kill you
- who sold you the idea of joining this network? Was it a trusted source and if so, does the person attend regularly?
- how efficient are the organisers of networking events? If they send out information in good time, proactively arrange business-related events, and understand the market, you have a good chance of benefiting from, and contributing to, the group.

When you are looking for a group to join, there are likely to be many factors that help you with the selection process — a bit like the £20,000 kitchen! As with Step 4, be as objective as you can, while taking note of the subjective factors. For example, the kitchen example in chapter 2 is a useful illustration here too: all the financial factors were the same, but it was the subjective element of rapport with the salesperson that made the difference. I belong to a breakfast networking group that generated 14% of my turnover in year one of trading. In addition, I have been given speaking opportunities that have been promotional for my business, been motivated by the group and their successes, as well as finding new business partnerships that would otherwise either not have been realised or have taken years to establish. For me, as well as the revenue stream, the culture of a group is extremely important. The culture is the subjective element here—find out what's important to you and look for it when joining new networks.

Common mistakes

✗ You join every group available

Enthusiasm is essential when you're networking, but do take care when you join groups. Make sure that they are all appropriate for you and your business and also check that you're not spreading yourself too thinly to attend all the meetings. Remember that you still have a business to run and you'll probably also have personal commitments to keep as well!

✗ You don't cut your losses

Sometimes, things just don't work out as planned; good networks dry up, your business focus changes, or you could just run out of time. If you find that you belong to a network to which you can no longer contribute, or which isn't helping you reach your goals, leave.

STEPS TO SUCCESS

✔ Measure up all your networking plans against your business plan.

✔ When you're thinking about which networking groups to join, be realistic. Don't take on too much or you'll end up bailing out and wasting money in the process.

✔ If possible, 'test' a network before you invest time and money in it. Ask the organisers if you can attend as a guest for a session or two so that you get a sense of what the meetings and attendees are like.

✔ Regularly measure the effectiveness of your networks.

✔ Unsubscribe from, or don't rejoin, groups that aren't helping you meet your goals.

Useful links

BNI:

www.bni-europe.com

Business Networking and Referrals:

www.brenet.co.uk

Chambers of Commerce online:

www.chamberonline.co.uk

Federation of Small Businesses:

www.fsb.org.uk

Microsoft (for a variety of Outlook and business contact solutions):

www.microsoft.com

Don't be a SLOB

With your business objectives clear in your mind and a highly organised contacts list, you can now enter the world of networking with confidence and professionalism. Networking *is* work— despite what your colleagues may say about your long lunches! You have quantified how valuable networking is to your business plan and success. Congratulations!

Hiding behind a business plan and networking strategy is no longer an option. You have the tools in place to make a success of your networking. With systems in place to suit your style, you can even enjoy the experience! This chapter shows you how to breeze through your first meeting, but the principles described below can be also be applied to social networking.

Step one: Look out for the danger signs

Four things can happen to a person when he or she is in a new or unfamiliar environment, whether it be a trip to the dentist, a job interview, or, in this case, networking. Recognising that these four things can happen gives you an opportunity to avoid them or deal with them professionally. They are:

1 **S**ense of humour failure. You get so caught up in the business of networking and achieving your goals that you forget to relax and make the most of the experience. Thanks to all your planning work, you already know you're at an event or on a website that will benefit your business, so why worry about the outcome? Go back to the worry chart in Chapter 1 and remind yourself that you can now only affect 8% of what you're worried about. You've planned the business approach to your networking; being yourself is going to be the subjective element. Allow yourself to be who you are and let your personality do the work.

2 **L**oss of memory. It's unlikely that networking will bring on a bout of amnesia, but we all forget things at times, especially if we're nervous. You may forget to meet with the people you had agreed to find, for example. If you know you are prone to forgetting things, write them down and take some notes with you so that you can refer to them during the event. Similarly, if you need to remember a date or place that a fellow networker mentions, don't be shy – write it down. It shows that you're genuinely interested, as well as making sure that you remember key information.

3 **O**dd or embarrassing behaviour is all too common if you're attempting to balance a plate of lunch, a glass of wine and a guest list at the same time as shaking hands with other networkers. And that's before you've rummaged around for a business card to exchange. Think ahead:

- lock your briefcase and valuables away so they aren't adding to the clutter
- don't arrive at an event ravenous with only food on your mind
- do you really need to knock back the wine as if it's going out of fashion?
- if you can't juggle, don't try. Nervous networkers need to reduce the likelihood of odd or embarrassing behaviour, not increase it. If you can find a seat and chat over lunch, there will be less room for cringing and more room for effective networking.

4 **B**ecoming breathless. Take deep breaths if you feel nervous. It's very easy for nerves to get the better of you if you're in a new or challenging situation, and often the body's response to that is to be short of breath. To our cave-dwelling ancestors, the fight/flight response was an essential tool for survival. Today, living as we do in very different environments, this is an ineffective reaction which can actively prevent us from responding usefully to a problem situation. Our non-essential processes are immediately switched off and we may feel our stomach churn (butterflies) or feel nauseous.

TOP TIP

Another common side effect of nerves is finding that you're speaking too quickly. If you feel as though you're babbling, you probably are, so pause and take a deep breath before resuming at a slower speed.

**It's fine to admit that you're nervous and
smile your way through it, too; honesty
is a great ice-breaker.**

Step two: Be yourself

Don't assume that you have to be an identikit business
person to succeed at networking. Being yourself is a really
powerful tool. Your company employs you for what you *can*
do, not for what you can't. Be open, honest, and friendly
when you meet people and they're much more likely to
respond in kind.

Step three: Be professional

You have to be on the ball mentally when you're preparing to
network, but you also have to make sure that you're looking
your best and are representing yourself and your business in
the most professional way possible. Make sure you have all
of the following under control:

✔ Your personal hygiene

- Clean, tidy hair
- Clean teeth and fresh breath
- Clean hands and fingernails
- A shower or bath every day as well as a clean shirt
  and socks
- A good brand of deodorant to combat both nerves
  and central heating.

✔ Your appearance

- You may be so confident that you don't think you have to follow the dress code, but you should. 'Black tie' usually means as much—be courteous to your host and respect their request. If you meet regularly in corporate offices there may well be a dress code there too. If in doubt, ask.
- Wear something comfortable as well as practical. This can be a particular challenge for women, as their jackets rarely have useful pockets, and bags add to the clutter. Try having 'networking trousers': left-hand pocket for incoming business cards, right for outgoing! Be creative and find a system that works for you.
- Do a full-length mirror check before you leave home or the office to be on the safe side.

✔ Your timing

- Be sure you leave space and time to travel, locate the venue, park, and arrive punctually and relaxed. It never ceases to amaze me how many people arrive late, leave early, grab a sandwich, and chat to a few old friends before rushing out again. Perhaps that was the objective; they are certainly not making the most of potential new contacts and are probably missing out on the possibilities with existing contacts.
- As you work your way through a networking event, be conscious of time and your objectives. Don't stress yourself about it; create awareness and the good habit of being time-conscious.

■ Allow yourself space to collect your thoughts. There is no need to rush around the room trying to shake every hand in the vicinity. The space you create will be particularly helpful if you aren't a seasoned networker.

Step four: Prepare for each specific event

Remember that the purpose of your networking is, in this case, work related. I once asked a chief executive what annoys him most about networking and he said, 'people who don't ask questions', so be warned! You know why you are there, but make sure you're clear about:

✔ Who you are going to meet and what you will ask them

✔ What *one* message you wish to get across or the information you are seeking

✔ Some points of reference in order that you can evaluate your networking after the event. Yes, you can include subjective comments in the evaluation too. What you can't do is hide behind them by saying things like 'it was great fun', 'it was a really motivating event', or 'it's definitely good for business!'.

Before an event, call the organiser and ask for a list of attendees in advance. If that's not available, ask for last month's list, as you can be sure that lots of people turn up regularly. If that tends not to happen, find out why (discreetly). If you haven't yet joined the group, is it going to help you make the most of your contacts if people appear once, never to return?

Take a few minutes to read through the list, looking for and noting contacts you know and contacts fitting your target client lists. These are the people you will look for and engage with. If you haven't been able to secure a list before the event, have the confidence to pick up the list on arrival, find a quiet corner, and do your pre-event trawling for five minutes.

At most face-to-face networking events you will be provided with some sort of ID badge. If you like your name and that of your company spelled correctly and looking professional, I urge you to brief the event organiser or bring your own ID badge. And please, if you wear a badge, ensure people can read it easily without having to stare at inappropriate parts of your anatomy.

Step five: Take a deep breath and dive in!

You've now prepared yourself in every way for professional networking. You have:

■ prepared your business plan in place (remember to keep it brief, one A4 page will do!)

- subscribed to relevant networks
- made time for the networking event
- dressed for the occasion
- trawled the guest list
- done your mirror check

The next section will most aid the nervous networkers among us. For serial networkers, take time to spot new people, welcome them and introduce them to others relevant to their business. This is your opportunity to contribute positively to the group.

✔ On arrival, register at the event and pick up and don your badge (or use your own).

✔ Explain that you are new, and if you don't know anyone on the list, ask to be pointed in the direction of one of your target contacts.

✔ If you recognise some names on the list, start there and move on.

✔ Take simple steps from one person to the next and don't be embarrassed to ask to be introduced to people. After all, that's what networking is about.

✔ Find somewhere to leave your valuables and free your hands for eating, drinking and shaking (and not because of the drink or nerves!).

✔ Look around the room and consider the layout. How will you work your way around most effectively?

✔ Find out the format of the event: when are the speeches? When does the food arrive?

Common mistakes

✗ You talk too much

You're networking to make contacts, so of course that means that you have to put your best foot forward and present yourself well. On the other hand, it doesn't mean that you have carte blanche to bang on about yourself or your favourite topic of conversation until you're blue in the face. Listen to what others are saying so that you can work out how best to help them—and how they can help you.

✗ You don't prepare

If you don't know what you're aiming to achieve, all your networking will be unfocused. You also won't be able to measure how successful you've been. Leave yourself plenty of time before the meeting to work out what you want to do and who you want to meet. Also, make sure that you're prepared in terms of your appearance. Do a quick mirror check before you go into the meeting and remember to have your business cards handy!

STEPS TO SUCCESS

✔ Keep your business objectives in mind.

✔ Be professional at all times: don't be a SLOB.

✔ Plan your first event carefully: make sure you know where to go and at what time. The more planning you do, the less stress you'll have on the day.

✔ Be aware of your personal hygiene and don't go over the top with perfume and aftershave.

Useful link

For more information about our flight/fight response:
www.helpishere.co.uk/fightflight.html

Stand and deliver

Being clear and concise when delivering your message is essential if you're trying to spread the word about you and your business. You need to be able to explain succinctly what it is that you do or want to achieve. This is often known as an 'elevator pitch': aim to describe your goals in the length of time it would take to travel a few floors in a lift with someone.

Step one: Think about the one-minute pitch carefully

Planning what you want to say when you introduce yourself to others or are given a chance to speak publicly requires some thought, particularly if you have a variety of products to promote. If you're confused, everyone else will be too.

Many networking groups offer people one minute in which to pitch their business. This may be weekly, monthly, or when you ask for a slot. Often you will be asked to speak at your first meeting—when you're likely to be the most nervous and unprepared. Even if you don't have a lot of public speaking experience, don't worry: one minute is completely doable if you spend some time preparing beforehand. Don't be put off by others who insist airily that they 'just wing it': probably a few lucky people do, but in the main all the good public speakers you hear will have prepared and practised what they want to say. (By the same token, you'll be able to spot those who haven't given it any thought at all as they drone on past the minute mark without delivering a single clear message.)

TOP TIP
Unless you prepare carefully, you'll waste 20 of the 60 seconds you've been allotted apologising for being nervous and unprepared. Focus on your message, not yourself!

Step two: Let *your* personality come through

There are as many ways of delivering a pitch as there are people—we all work in different ways. Although it's helpful to follow good practice that you see in others, don't tailor your presentation in such a way that you sound the same as everyone else. It's important to be yourself when speaking in public.

As you gain confidence, you'll be able to try new ways of delivering your message. Know your own limits, though, and don't try to be a comedian if you aren't one. Timing is everything, and if you waste 30 seconds of 60 telling a joke that falls flat, your confidence will plummet. Add to that the

20 seconds you spend apologising for being nervous and unprepared and you have just 10 seconds left to deliver a meaningful message. So not only is your self-belief in shreds, but your professional image has taken a bit of a bash too.

For most people, standing up in front of a crowd of strangers to speak is the most terrifying part about networking. The good news is that with practice and preparation you can overcome the fear and even look forward to speaking up. As with most other aspects of business, it's easier to move out of your comfort zone if you have others working with you. So if this is an area you want to develop, enlist some help and positive support. If you have a mentor or coach, ask him or her to work with you on this issue. If your budget doesn't stretch to that, ask a trusted friend, colleague, or family member to listen to you practise.

Step three: Sharpen your focus

Now's the time to establish a clear focus for your talk. Every business has different needs, of course, but the main question to answer here is the same for everyone: what **one** thing do you want to get across to your audience? It may take some time to pin this down, but no matter; once you are clear about this, so will your audience be. If other people are going to do business with you or refer to their own contacts, they must have one thing to remember.

There is an easy way to do this. Let's say you have 12 things that you want to get across when you speak. You're not

going to be able to cram them all into one minute, so pace
yourself. Aim to tackle each of the 12 issues one at a time
over a number of meetings or events. Some suggestions
about how to do this are shown in the table below;
these can be combined and adapted to suit your
business.

Tax-year end products	Seasonal products, such as diaries or calendars
New Year sale	New product
Special offers	Book launch
Business tip for a specific audience	Introductory offer
Christmas sale	News announcement
Seminars x 4 per year	Client testimonial

If you try to sell your new product at the same time as
launching a seminar and offering Summer Sale
opportunities, you'll probably confuse your audience as well
as yourself. Most networkers want to help one another, so
make it easy for them.

Step four: Consider who you are looking for

By now you should know the one message you want to get
across in your one-minute pitch. Just as you have targeted
the most relevant networking events to join, you now need
to establish your specific target audience—the people you

want to reach. Remember, a wide audience is listening and you are trying to find the right people for your business from yours and others' spheres of contact. In considering your target audience for the selected product to promote, think of a coffee filter system. The coffee beans have to be ground to a manageable size for the filter. Then there are three different 'sieve' sizes that filter the coffee to its final, delicious format. You need to do the same with your target audience so that they know exactly who you are looking for as well as what you are asking for.

Step five: Prepare your delivery

Preparing well is the best way of making a positive impact when you speak. Think about the following key points when you're gearing up for your one-minute spot.

Event format
- Is it a formal or informal gathering? Are you expecting 20 or 200 people? Think about the acoustics of where you'll be speaking. If you are in a roomful of 200 people, you're probably going to need a microphone to get yourself heard.
- Is it your first time at the event or are you and your business well known? Even though many people may know you well, there are bound to be newcomers to an event. Don't assume that people will know who you are, even if you move in a relatively small circle. A little humility goes a long way, and it's better to be pleasantly surprised by the number of people who know you.

Perceptions of your business

- Avoid industry terminology or acronyms that require long explanations If at all possible.

- Think about how you use your corporate strapline. There are as many pitfalls around straplines as there are uses for them. Used wisely, they work well as a way of making people remember you. A fun example is an office products company I know, whose managing director uses two straplines. One comes at the start of his pitch: 'ISIS Office Products and Print. We supply office products and print'; and one after his pitch: 'Keeping stationery on the move!' They both work because they are delivered well and regularly, to the extent that the members of the group have been known to join in! The dry humour is understood and suits the MD's style. Cheesy straplines won't work positively for everyone.

Learn from others

- Watch and listen to other people as they do their one-minute pitch. What works? What doesn't work? How can you adapt the parts that *do* work to suit your business? What did you remember? Why? What made you take action as a result of their pitch?

- Talk to people who present well and ask about their networking skills and what impact they have on their business.

- If you're a very nervous presenter, swallow your pride and—no matter how senior you are in your company—invest in some public speaking training. You will benefit from coaching or training on a one-to-one basis.

Be audible

✔ Make sure people can hear you. If possible, plant a friend or colleague at the back of the room and ask them to raise their hand if they can't hear. Failing that, quietly ask someone to assist you with this before it's your turn to speak. If the acoustics are bad but event venues rotate, consider not speaking at all that day. Wait until a venue with good acoustics or a microphone comes up.

✔ Part of being heard is about confidence. When you know what you are saying, you can stand up straight, look at the audience, and project your voice clearly.

✔ Practice makes perfect. Sixty seconds is no time at all when you're feeling confident, but can seem like a lifetime if you're nervous. So practise your speech in front of a mirror, in front of a colleague—whatever gives you the most confidence.

✔ If you have to use a microphone, don't blow into it to see if it's working. Tapping it is a bit antiquated too. Step close to it; ignore it; look at your audience and speak slowly and clearly. You are unlikely to be the first to use the microphone, so watch the others who go first, observing where they stood to be heard clearly.

✔ If you haven't heard the previous speakers clearly when they've used the microphone, check the system with the master of ceremonies and don't speak until you are sure you can be heard.

Handling nerves

✔ Most people are nervous to some degree or other before speaking in public, so don't be hard on yourself if nerves affect you. You're not alone!

✔ Drink water before speaking, rather than anything stronger.

✔ People often speak very quickly when they're nervous, so be aware of this and slow down if you need to. Time yourself when practising.

Notes

✔ For a one-minute presentation, you should be able to manage with either no notes or just some brief bullet points. For example:

- Name/Company
- Thought-provoking question or statement to grab attention
- Product or service that your company is offering
- Target audience you're looking for
- Corporate strapline, if you have one
- Name/Company
- Thank you

Substitutes

✔ If someone is standing in for you at an event and they are likely to be asked to speak on your behalf, be sure to choose someone who will represent you professionally.

✔ Brief them fully about your product and any specific offering you are announcing.

✔ Give them bullet-point notes to guide their presentation.

✔ Make sure that the event organisers know someone is standing in for you.

✔ Think about asking a trusted client to give a testimonial about your company. Their words will be a valuable sales pitch in themselves.

✔ Listen carefully to your replacement's feedback after the event. They're likely to meet a different group of people to you and may well see possibilities within the group that you have missed before.

Common mistakes

✗ You think you can wing it

Honestly, you can't. Respect your audience and do the best job you can for them as well as for you. Check your business plan so that you're very clear on what you want to say and then practise until you feel comfortable. Time yourself too, so that you're not flapping about talking for too long.

STEPS TO SUCCESS

✔ When you're presenting, learn from those around you but don't mimic them.

✔ Practise as much as you need to make sure you're comfortable with your speech.

✔ Dress appropriately for the occasion. Keep it simple but smart if you're unsure about what to wear.

✔ Find out as much as you can beforehand about what type of venue it is, whether the meeting is informal or formal, and how many people are due to attend.

✔ If you're worried about not being heard, ask a friend or colleague to sit at the back of the room so that he or she can give you a discreet signal if you're too quiet.

Useful links

BBC (search for 'presentation skills'):
www.bbc.co.uk
Executive Solutions:
www.executive-solutions.co.uk
Google (click on 'Images' option):
www.google.co.uk

Confident networking

This chapter will enable you to move your networking to the next level for your own set of circumstances. There will also be an opportunity for you to prepare a longer presentation about your business as an extension to your one-minute pitch. We all have different levels of confidence and unless we stretch ourselves we'll never find out what we're really capable of. You may well have hit all your business targets and be quite happy with your contacts and the relationships you have with them. That's great, but why not challenge yourself to reach out for new and potentially even more fruitful possibilities? Everyone reaches a plateau at some point, but it's good to keep striving so that you're continually contributing effectively to your existing networks as well as building new ones.

Step one: Find your blind spots

You're probably familiar with your physical blind spot when driving: that moment when an overtaking car can't be seen in any of your mirrors. In other senses, though, a blind spot is an area or facet of one's personality of which one remains ignorant or fails to gain understanding. If you're already a confident networker, finding and accepting that you have a blind spot may be quite a challenge, but it's worth taking a close, critical look at your networking skills.

To do this, ask a colleague or friend to help you to assess where you are with your networking and whether you are making the most of your contacts. You must be prepared to let him or her ask you searching questions and be ready to heard some unvarnished truths.

When you're ready to take the plunge, take your colleague through your one-page business plan together with the table showing the networking groups you belong to. Show them your networking rationale and ask them to review it with you. This is where their objectivity will really come into play. Can they spot any holes in your plan? Are there any target networks they can see that you've not spotted thus far?

Exercise

Think of someone whose networking style you admire. If you're a nervous networker, ask the other person if he or she would be willing to mentor you until you're feeling more confident about networking.

If you're already feeling comfortable about networking and want to move up a gear, find someone who will stretch you out of your comfort zone. You may actually need a coach rather than a mentor: a coach will not necessarily work in the same field of business as you, while a mentor will pass on experience or knowledge with possibilities for door opening. A good coach will focus on setting and achieving goals within specific timescales, as well as stretching you to reach out of your comfort zone. Be sure you understand the difference between the two before making an investment in your networking by having a coach.

- Be clear about what you are asking and what success will 'look like' for you.
- Be open to his or her suggestions: if you're not very good at receiving feedback, you'll be wasting a lot of time and money.
- Be prepared to try new things.
- Explain your business plan and how networking fits in overall.
- Make sure you have a schedule in mind so that both you and your coach or mentor know what needs to be achieved and when.

Step two: Present your business to fellow networkers

One of the benefits of meeting people regularly in a networking group is that you can learn about each other's business as well as explaining your own main activities. This exchange of information enables you and others to find, give, and receive the most relevant tips, leads, and referrals. Don't make assumptions about other people's knowledge of your company—no one knows it as well as you do!—and if you absolutely have to use acronyms, explain them. For example, stating boldly that you're a member of the AA is fine, but acquaintances could be struggling to work out whether you belong to the Automobile Association, Alcoholics Anonymous, or the Advertising Association. If in doubt, spell it out.

In Chapter 6 we looked at useful ways to prepare for a one-minute presentation. As you become more practised and better known to your networking groups, you may be asked to give up to a ten-minute presentation about your business. This is an ideal forum for telling people more about yourself and your business—your goals and aspirations. You can also mention challenges you're encountering while you're in this environment; you never know who in the audience may be able to help and advise.

TOP TIP
Don't by shy! If others are speaking regularly and you haven't been offered a speaking slot, ask for one.

The following tips are an outline that you will find useful as you prepare, plan, and practise a longer presentation. Use this opportunity to reach the next level in making the most of your contacts. We covered some of these key elements in Chapter 6, but remember to:

1. **Prepare thoroughly.** You want people to understand how your business ticks, so take the time to prepare

your material and stay focused. Refer back to your A4 business plan from Chapter 2 so that you have your business challenges and targets uppermost in your mind. Part of building trusted business relationships involves a degree of vulnerability, but don't feel you have to bang on about problems: ask targeted questions that refer to what you want to achieve, but frame it positively. For example: 'My goal is to have 10% of my turnover from the retail sector in the next eight months. What experience or ideas do you have that can take me there?'

2. **Be true to your own style.** Be true to who *you* are and value what you and your business are offering. Deliver your presentation in a style that works for you. We've already seen that 'people buy people', so now is your opportunity to be professional but genuine.

3. **Know your business and focus on it.** Familiarise yourself with all the ins and outs of your business. Take a fine toothcomb to your business plan, working with a colleague if that's helpful, and imagine *you* are listening to the presentation. What would you ask if you were in the audience? Brainstorm the questions; categorise them; focus on the main subjects and answer the questions in your presentation. If you truly can't answer them, ask the question in the presentation and see what your networking colleagues come up with.

As you want to spread the word about what you do, think about the following key areas. Remember to focus only on relevant information and those things your networking colleagues need to help them understand your business.

- **Your professional background/credentials.** This section of your presentation acts as a tool for others to see that you can be trusted, and will help to build relationships. If it will be helpful in painting a picture of your business, and will include industry organisations you belong to and professional accreditations.
- **Your main functions/products.** You won't have time to explain the fabulous benefits of every product down to the last widget. Select one or two that you're currently focusing on and for which you'll be looking for referrals.
- **The role of your network.** Try to illustrate how your networking group has helped you develop your business, as shown below. Or if you are new, be clear on your expectations of the group and your own contribution.

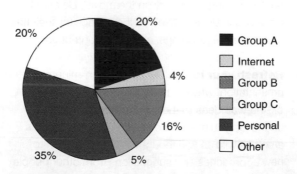

Source of business

Group A	20%
Internet	4%
Group B	16%
Group C	5%
Personal	35%
Other	20%

■ **Future business goals/targets.** Your networking group will be able to support your weekly requests if they understand your long-term objectives. Let them know what you are looking for in the longer term and how you see the networking group contributing to that. You then have the basis for future presentations, when you can update and add relevant information.

4. **Practise** your presentation so that you don't have to read reams of notes. (If you feel that you do need a memory prompt, note down some bullet points on small cards.) Ask a colleague to give you feedback and remember to check your timing as well as the relevance of the content.

5. **The one thing!** What is the one thing you want people to remember about your business for future referrals? To hammer it home, you could repeat your company's strapline at the end of you presentation: 'executive business coaching—making your business more productive, fun, and profitable'; or 'office products and print—keeping stationery on the move'. Be sure to close positively and thank your audience for their time and, if they've given one, a positive contribution.

6. **Refresh your ideas.** During your ten-minute presentation, why not bring some of your more off-the-wall ideas to the table? With fresh brains on the job you may discover some of your dreams aren't as wild as you thought. Always be open to new approaches and suggestions from other people

too. Not everyone will agree with you, but during the course of conversation an even better option or approach may present itself.

7. **Don't be scuppered by technology.** Plan well in advance if you are using technology as part of your presentation. Phone ahead to the venue to check that all the facilities you need will be easily accessible. Also, arrive early to set up so that there are no painful silences while you scrabble around on the floor under a desk looking for a plug socket. If you're not 100% confident about the technology you want to use, this isn't the time to practise. Leave it at home!

Death by PowerPoint

PowerPoint can be a really useful addition to presentations. It's best to keep things simple, though, for maximum effect.

- Be sparing with the flying words and zany backgrounds. As with your business, focus, clarity, and simplicity are the keys to success.
- Adapt your corporate colours and use logos wisely. Use the Master slide to set up your template.
- Less is more. Don't fill the screen with too much text. Highlight key issues with bullet points that carry the bare bones of your message; you can elaborate when you're speaking.
- If you have more than 20 slides, you won't be able to present in less than ten minutes unless you whizz through at top speed, thereby confusing the listener.

■ Ask for help if you need it. If you aren't confident, learn
from other, trusted presenters as you prepare your
presentation. Failing that, PowerPoint offers some
helpful advice with either the Office Assistant or the
Help button. Use it as a resource that you can tap
into on- or off-line.

8. **Think about using some personal information.**
Networking brings people together, so it is fine to show
that you're not a robot! Your introduction can explain to
the group who you are and what makes you tick—and
if it's an early morning meeting, some light relief too!
Family photos, holiday or other photos will show
people *who* you are. You could also bring an unusual
fact about yourself to the table. A networking colleague
of mine opened his presentation with his charitable
work for raising testicular cancer awareness and his
personal experience. I had to present to a new group
on my birthday, so I included a baby picture and three
others from my life history. Be creative and use
anniversaries or memorable dates to set the scene. This
is one slide I used when presenting on my birthday:

Clifton Consulting
Established in 1959

Step three: Learn to stretch yourself

As your confidence builds, you can start to look for new areas of networking and experiment with different ways of operating. If you are a successful e-networker, how about trying some face-to-face networking? You may discover new opportunities and skills that you've missed up till now. If you plan sensibly and make the most of your time, you've got nothing to lose by at least trying some new networking opportunities. As long as you assess progress and costs, taking one step at a time, you'll be fine.

With a mentor or coach as encouragement, you'll have some pleasant surprises. By changing one thing at a time, you'll be able to monitor outcomes as they appear, assess them and make permanent changes that enable you to make the most of your contacts. Let's say you decide to go to fewer networking groups. Drop them one at a time, rather than all in one go, so that you can assess the impact as groups fall off your radar. The same applies if you decide to take on more groups: be sure to quantify their success before you move on or drop them. Perhaps there are industry special interest groups you've been considering but never bothered to take the plunge? Now is the time!

Common mistakes

✗ You become complacent

If you've been networking for a while, or if you're a relative newcomer now in a comfortable groove, it's very easy to stop putting in the effort. What you put in is definitely rewarded by what you get back out, however, so take time to regularly review what you aim to achieve in your networking efforts. Business goals can change quite radically, often at short notice, so make sure that your efforts are going in the right direction.

✗ You don't want to share your business challenges with other members of your networking group

We all want to come across to contacts and acquaintances as successful and capable. Sharing business concerns with your networking group doesn't make them look down on you in any respect: it's likely that most of the other people in the room will have had a similar experience. Phrase your question or share your concern positively and you're much more likely to get a positive response in return.

STEPS TO SUCCESS

 Review your networking 'blind spots'. It's a good way of reviewing progress and setting future goals.

✔ Good networkers want to support one another. Be as ready to contribute to other people's presentations as you are keen for them to contribute to yours.

✔ If you want something, ask for it! If no-one knows that you need something, how can they help you?

Useful links

Clifton Consulting:
www.cliftonconsulting.com
International Coach Federation:
www.coachfederation.org

Following up with contacts after an event

Now that you're confident about getting out there and meeting people at networking events, remember to follow up properly afterwards so that you can turn a good conversation into a good business relationship. Putting together a comprehensive and practical contacts list is a crucial part of this. Review it regularly to refresh your contacts and database. If you don't organise your contacts, you'll lose sales and marketing opportunities, which will in turn slow your progress towards your business goals. I used to work for a dynamic sales director whose first rule of success was to 'get organised!'

Step one: Build your contacts

Exercise

1. Revisit your list of target clients and see if there are any emerging patterns that can help as you organise your contacts—for example, categories of business; or clients who regularly refer business to you or for whom you supply referrals. By doing this, you may find new areas to network.

> **2.** Collect together all the business cards, leaflets, scraps of paper, and jottings with contact names that are lying around your desk or in your briefcase or wallet. Add these now to your official contact list. If you really can't do it today, put a realistic time and date in your diary for doing so . . . and stick to it.

If you've completed all the exercises in the book so far, you'll be in a strong position to set up an effective contact system. In Chapter 4 we looked at the importance of being organised as a networker. Now is the time to work out the best system for *your* style and *your* business needs. If you work in an organisation, you could benefit from an existing company database. Alternatively, you may need to work around an existing company database or customer relationship management (CRM) system. If you run your own company, you could create one from scratch if you wanted to. There are hundreds of CRM systems available on the market, but before you venture into spending vast sums of money on one, thoroughly understand your business needs and the return on investment you expect from such a system. For some excellent guidance on how to approach CRM, visit the Business Link and Chartered Institute of Marketing websites listed at the end of this chapter.

Below are some suggestions of systems you can use. Keep it simple at first and then work up to more advanced systems if you want to. If you start off with everything being too complicated, you'll quickly run out of steam and your contact list will become out of date very quickly.

✔ Use Microsoft Outlook to organise your contacts.

✔ Keep business cards in an index book or box. Keep it
    tidy and order them alphabetically in some way, either by
    surname of the person or by business name. If you work
    with others, keep the index box somewhere prominent in
    your office or on your desk so that your colleagues can
    find this useful information.

✔ Use your company's or your personal database to
    update contacts and keep notes. If you are don't know
    how to use a database, ask for training.

Step two: Decide what information you are going to store

Networking events come around faster than expected; if you
update your database after each event, you'll be able to keep
track of who's who and what you have discussed or agreed.
You can then make the most of your contacts. Deciding
what information you are going to store will be dependent
upon your business needs and the database you use. In
addition to relevant business information, some of us like to
remember birthdays, family members' names and other
such personal information. That may sound pretty Big
Brother-like, but if you genuinely want to remember and build
relationships, writing down information may be your best
way of remembering and caring. Whatever you decide to
store, you must be aware of the Data Protection Act: do *not*

add your contacts to third-party mailing lists without their prior knowledge.

Exercise

Take a few moments to answer the following questions:

- How out of date is your business card filing system?
- When (specific date) are you going to update your business card filing system/networking database?
- Who are you going to work with on this project?

The reason I've suggested you do this exercise is that unless you take the time to update your system, you'll never get the best from it. Working with another person on the project will enable you to articulate your goals, brainstorm new ideas, and keep the momentum going. Championship tennis players and top golfers often mislead us into thinking that their game comes naturally and easily. The effort and practice they put into their successes would make the strongest of us go weak at the knees. As with sport, you need effort and organisation to benefit from your networking.

Step three: Build a routine

Once you've accepted a business card you need to do something positive with it. Do think carefully about the people from whom you accept business cards. If I think that people randomly take my business card with no intention of doing anything other than eventually putting it in the bin, I'd rather not give them a card at all. Whether or not you like what's going on around you, it's perfectly possible for you to set your own standards of good practice. If you do, it's you and your business that will benefit, as well as those you are in contact with.

✔ If you know you want to keep in contact with someone you've met while you've been networking, make it a rule to follow up within 24 hours.

✔ Decide on how you want to follow up. You could write a brief note, send an e-mail or make a quick phone call. You'll soon find out if this is the beginning of a trusted working relationship.

✔ Having followed up, decide how you are going to make the most of this particular contact in the short, medium, and long term. For example, you could set up a meeting; send more information; write an article; or add them to your Top Tips mailing list.

✔ Don't just throw a pile of business cards at your assistant and ask him or her to put them into your database: what good is that? You need to delegate properly to your assistant by explaining what you want to achieve and giving him or her the freedom to organise your database. They will support you in this exercise and may suggest a better, improved system!

Step four: Rise above the clutter

Every day we are bombarded with e-mails from sources both known and unknown. The danger is that these e-mails become like wallpaper and fade into the background. So many people mark even the most innocuous messages as 'urgent' and are unclear about what they want that it can be difficult to work out exactly what needs most attention.

If you want people to sit up and take notice of you, you'll need to stand out from the crowd. Think about the high street and about how the many different stores differentiate themselves: John Lewis have their Partner system and their famous slogan, 'never knowingly undersold'; Argos has its catalogue system and low overheads; the Co-op has its focus on the environment and fair trading. How are *you* and your business going to differentiate yourselves? For example, could you list any of these?

- Your ability to listen to others and meet their needs, rather than bombarding them purely with what you want to sell to them
- Your pricing structure
- Your unique selling point (USP)
- The personalities in your business
- Your returns policy
- Your customer service
- Some or all of the above.

It isn't difficult to stand out when following up from networking events as over 80% of people don't even bother. Recently I followed up a meeting with a letter and hard copy of my seminar notes. It wasn't difficult or time-consuming to do; yet the personal touch was well received, and remembered: the recipient made a positive comment about it the next time we met.

Step five: Let your business card do the work

After you've left a room, your business card will stay behind and, if it's designed well, can work on your behalf. Take a long, dispassionate look at it. Does it need to change to reflect you and your company better? Or does it just need an update? Notice what people say when they receive your card; pick up on positive comments and use them wisely next time you redesign. These days it needn't be expensive to design and print cards online or at a printer's. Get the best-quality one your budget can stand; it will serve you well.

- Your business card is part of your business brand and completes the picture of you as well as your company. Does your current business card offer a true reflection of your brand?
- Is there space to write on your business card? People often want to write notes on cards that can act as an aide-mémoire. I've even seen a card with specific spaces allocated for comments such as those shown below:

```
We met at _____

We discussed _____

We agreed to meet on / at

        _____
```

Step six: Keep the momentum going

Networking should be a daily activity, interspersed with specific events. Keep up the momentum of ideas and meetings going forward. You can do this by writing things down, agreeing specific deadlines and activities. Don't rely on others to keep an idea alive: it's great if they do, of course, but be proactive, take the initiative, and move forward, bringing colleagues with you.

Networking doesn't only happen at special events; your spheres of contact are continuously growing and overlapping. Review them regularly and look for networking opportunities 'in disguise'. For example, attending a training course or public meeting won't necessarily be advertised as a networking opportunity but it certainly is. Take an interest in those around you; learn about their business and look for opportunities to build trusted relationships that can benefit you both.

Above all, be professional in your approach and appearance. At the beginning of the book I challenged you to enjoy the experience of networking. With your business plan to hand, your one-minute pitch prepared, and some great networking opportunities to seize, I wish you much fun and every success!

Common mistakes

✗ You don't organise and update your list of contacts

Keeping on top of the business cards you'll receive at networking events can be time-consuming at first, but it's well worth it. You don't need a complicated or expensive system to do this—index cards, your e-mail contacts option or even an Excel spreadsheet would do—but you do need to come up with a system that works for you and then stick to it. If you have an assistant, ask him or her to help you out with this.

✗ You don't follow up

Following up when you meet someone at a networking event means that you're much more likely to get your business relationship off to a good start. Follow up as soon as you can so that your conversation is still relatively fresh in your mind and try as best you can to do so in a way that will help your new contact. They'll notice your thoughtfulness.

✗ You 'make do' with your business card

The way your business card looks probably isn't at the top of your list of priorities. That's fair enough, but when you start to network, you need to make sure that your card carries on working when you leave the room. Make sure that it ties in well with your company branding and that all the details are up to date; if they're not, get a new one designed. Scribbling your new phone number or e-mail address over the old one does not look good!

STEPS TO SUCCESS

✔ Follow up promptly with good potential contacts. It's the best way to start off a business relationship.

✔ Be thorough and relevant with your follow-up.

✔ Take the time to personalise any communication you have with new contacts.

✔ Make sure your business card looks professional and is completely up to date.

Useful links

Business Link:

www.businesslink.gov.uk (for information about data protection look at the IT and e-commerce page)

Chartered Institute of Marketing:

www.cim.co.uk

The last word . . .

No matter how hard your business card works for you, it can't replace you and the impression you project. Part of that overall impression is how true you are to your word. If you say your company will deliver a product or service to a particular standard or time-frame, it's essential that you do that. To make the most of your contacts, you must become known as a person or company who delivers what they promise. Also remember that networking is for the mutual benefit of those in a group, and with that in mind, participate fully in both formal and social activities.